Documenting Defold Programm

OCR A Level Computer Science

D Hillyard
C Sargent

Published by
CRAIGNDAVE LTD
12 Tweenbrook Avenue
Gloucester
Gloucestershire
GL1 5JY
United Kingdom

admin@craigndave.co.uk
www.craigndave.org

Craig 'n' Dave

Edited by A. Fenn
Graphics and typesetting by CraignDave Ltd
First edition 2020

ISBN: 9798649775151

A copy of this book is held in the British Library.

About the authors

David Hillyard

David is a postgraduate-qualified teacher with a Bachelor of Science (Honours) in Computing with Business Information Technology. David has over twenty years' teaching experience in ICT and computing in four comprehensive schools and one grammar school in Cheltenham, Gloucestershire. He has been an assistant headteacher, head of department, chair of governors and founding member of a multi-academy trust of primary schools.

Formerly subject leader for the Gloucestershire Initial Teacher Education Partnership (GITEP) at the University of Gloucestershire, David has successfully led a team of PGCE/GTP mentors across the county. His industry experience includes programming for the Ministry of Defence. A self-taught programmer, he wrote his first computer game at ten years old.

Craig Sargent

Craig is a postgraduate-qualified teacher with a Bachelor of Science (Honours) in Computer Science with Geography. Craig has over fourteen years' teaching experience in ICT and computing in a large comprehensive school in Stroud, Gloucestershire, at a grammar school and as a private tutor. A head of department, examiner and moderator for awarding bodies in England, Craig has authored many teaching resources for major publishers.

He also previously held roles as a Computing at School (CAS) Master Teacher and regional coordinator for the Computing Network of Excellence. His industry experience includes freelance contracting for a large high street bank and programming for the Ministry of Defence. He also wrote his first computer game in primary school.

Both Craig and Dave have decades of experience delivering A Level Computer Science projects, and their students' work is consistently commended year after year without adjustment from the examination board moderators.

Foreword

I got a Commodore 64 at a relatively young age, and like all the other kids, I played a lot of games. The C64 also came with a ring-bound manual for the Basic programming language that fascinated me. For some reason, I can still remember the smell of the pages, the excitement of trying to understand what it all meant and the joy when a typed-in program ran for the first time.

This feeling of excitement never really left me, and I brought it with me to the Amiga where I learned the Motorola assembly language and started creating games and demos for real. The tools available back then are a far cry from the engines and creation tools that exist today, but the joy of seeing your creation running on a mobile phone or a browser using modern tools is the same as I felt back then.

Mixing a formal Computer Science education with a genuine interest in game development and problem-solving will help you get a foot in the industry. Learn the theory, but do not forget to also put in the hours in front of the computer, hacking away on games, participating in game jams and experimenting with different technologies.

Defold is a great place to start your journey into game design. It is a completely free-to-use engine for the development of desktop, mobile and web games. Game logic is written in Lua, with the option to use native code to extend the engine with additional functionality. Defold is used by a growing number of developers to create commercial hits, being praised for its ease of use, technical documentation and a very friendly community of developers.

There are no ready-made complex components available in Defold, making it ideal for your Computer Science project. Instead, we believe the job of Defold is to empower game developers with simple, powerful collaborative tools.

Enjoy!

Björn Ritzl, Product Owner, Defold Foundation

Contents

INITIAL IDEAS

There are specific examination board requirements you should be aware of before you start your project. It is also important to scope your project to ensure it is manageable in the time you have available.

Choosing a project

One of the considerations when embarking on a programming project with Defold is ensuring you choose a game with sufficient complexity to be of A Level standard; this is not easy to define, but it must be more complex than typical GCSE work. As a minimum, it must include:

- a graphical user interface; and
- complex algorithms.

Most video games, by their very nature, have a graphical user interface. You can see graphics on the screen. That does not mean your interface must also include the classic GUI controls or WIMPS (windows, icons, menus, pointers). It is perfectly acceptable to have any suitable input mechanism and output. However, the game must include some graphics and at least a couple of different screens. Minimally, there should be a landing screen once the game loads and a screen to play the game on.

There are no marks for graphics themselves, so you should not spend too much time creating artwork. It is acceptable to source and use sprite sheets (collections of graphics) for your game, providing you reference your sources and do not sell your game commercially.

To be considered complex, your game will typically include the use of standard algorithms. Defold already has engines for collision detection, physics and particle effects, so you will gain little credit for these. Instead, you need to look for other requirements such as maze generation, sorting (for a high score table) or pathfinding for enemy AI. These are just examples, not specific requirements.

A* TOP TIP

Retro 2D games that were popular in the 1980s are great reference material for ideas. Iterating an old game can be fun – and about the right complexity too.

Consider the complexity of the algorithms you study on the A Level Computer Science course as a benchmark. These include linear search, binary search, bubble sort, insertion sort, merge sort, quick sort, Dijkstra and A* algorithm. You are unlikely to need many of these, but they give you an idea of the level of complexity required.

A game of noughts and crosses where a player simply chooses a grid position to place their mark is more like a GCSE project – in other words, not complex enough. However, including an algorithm that demonstrates machine learning such as MENACE (Machine Educable Noughts and Crosses Engine) would turn this into a great A Level project. A simple game of battleships where the computer opponent chooses a random square to fire at is simplistic. An algorithm that decides the next position to fire on after a hit is scored and is dependent on the shape of ships already shot down has that added layer of complexity that would elevate the project to A Level standard.

A game of Pong with two paddles and a ball is too simplistic because Defold will do too much of the work for you, leaving little code for you to write. Extending this to a breakout clone with bricks and power-ups adds the required complexity. Extending this further into a four-player version where players defend their castle in the four corners of the screen like the classic Atari game *Warlords* would be fantastic. It is usually possible to take a simple idea and, through a series of extensions, arrive at a game with sufficient complexity.

Getting the scope right

An achievable, well-written project is usually better than an over-ambitious, incomplete and poorly written one. That said, it is important to set yourself a challenge so that you have enough to write about when it comes to justifying your approaches. Deciding what you will attempt and what will remain beyond the objectives of the project is known as *scope* in software engineering.

Some games are more complex to make than others. Remember, AAA games are developed by large teams working full-time over several years. You are on your own and have a short amount of time. Recreating and building upon 2D retro games of the 1980s is a far better proposition than a modern-day 3D first-person shooter. One of the most popular and successful games in recent times was *Candy Crush*. It was also one of the simplest.

Sometimes, what appears complex can be straightforward. For example, Defold offers the developer a fully integrated physics engine with limited coding requirements; this makes games such as *Angry Birds* simpler to implement than they might appear at first. When scoping your project, begin by learning and understanding the capabilities of Defold in advance and consider how you will build the required complexity into your development.

It is important that, while you stretch yourself, you do not take on a completely unachievable project. With many classic games, it is often easy to scale them back to reduce the scope.

The table on the next page will help you conclude where compromises could be made. If your game sits entirely in the left-hand column of the table, you probably do not have enough complexity. If your project is mostly in the right-hand column, perhaps you have too much complexity.

When scoping your project, consider how you might shift the emphasis of each aspect left or right to balance complexity against what is achievable.

Examiner's advice

"The best projects tend to be more ambitious. Candidates need to have enough scope to develop their game over several iterations. A project that a candidate can complete without encountering any challenges will give them little to write about. Conversely, a candidate can still receive high marks for an ambitious project that does not achieve all its aims.

Helping to scope your project

Easier to implement		**Harder to implement**
Single screen - e.g., *Space Invaders, Pac-Man*	Multiple single screens - e.g., *Bomb Jack, Bubble Bobble*	Fully scrolling with camera - e.g., *Super Mario, Gauntlet*
One type of enemy	A few different enemies	Lots of different enemies
No enemy AI - e.g., *Space Invaders*	Simple enemy AI - e.g., *Pac-Man*	Intelligent enemy AI - e.g., *Killzone*
Single life	Multiple lives or health	Combination of health and lives
No animations - e.g., static images, player's ship in *Space Invaders*	Changing images - e.g., movement sprites walking left and right	Physics objects - e.g., rolling dice tumbling in 3D
A single level	A couple of levels	Multiple levels with a boss fight
Levels with no platforms/walls	Levels with horizontal platforms and vertical walls	Angled or moving platforms
Two-player	Single-player with bots	Networked multiplayer
Static background	Moving background	Parallax scrolling
Horizontal/vertical movement and single-direction firing	Eight-way movement and firing	Full rotational movement and firing
No changeable settings	Simple settings - e.g., volume control	Advanced settings - e.g., changing difficulty level
All data is stored within the project	Use of external modules to build data or function libraries	Use of JSON to load and store external data
Simple sound effects	Conditional sound effects	Dynamic sound

Using Defold

The examination board provide a list of approved programming languages that students may use. Defold is an integrated development environment (IDE) for the Lua programming language in the same way that Visual Studio is an IDE for C#. That is why Defold does not appear in the approved list of languages. Lua is an approved language, and developments using the Defold IDE are acceptable programming projects for A Level.

Your teacher does not need to be familiar with Defold or Lua. You will be describing your algorithms, providing pseudocode, commenting your source code and explaining how you developed your coded solution. There should be enough detail in your writing for your teacher to understand your code and mark your work effectively, even if they cannot develop in Lua themselves.

> A* TOP TIP
>
> It is not necessary for your teacher to be able to code in Lua – it is unlikely the examiner can either! Your project will need to include detailed explanations of the algorithms you have written.

There is a misconception that students are required to use object-oriented techniques to ensure their project has sufficient complexity. There is no requirement to use a specific programming paradigm. Indeed, it is possible to write a simplistic object-oriented program that would not be sufficient for A Level. OOP alone does not make a project complex. Lua is an imperative language and is not truly object-oriented. However, Defold's implementation of Lua requires many of the object-oriented principles such as instances, encapsulation and message passing. It also makes extensive use of many of the concepts you are taught during the course. One example is the use of hashing. These are great talking points when justifying approaches to gain high marks in your project.

> A* TOP TIP
>
> Use features of an IDE or language that are available and do not rewrite algorithms already provided. However, your development must include plenty of original code too.

There is no requirement for you to write unnecessary code. For example, Defold handles collision detection already, so there is no need for you to code an algorithm for that. Good projects will make appropriate use of the facilities of the IDE - that is how real software is developed!

At A Level, if you rely too much on library code, you risk limiting your opportunity to provide evidence of code you have written. There should be a good balance between making use of built-in functionality and writing your own algorithms.

> **A* TOP TIP**
>
> Do not fall into the trap of thinking the code is the most important part of this work. It is worth up to 25 marks, but there are 70 available in total – the report accounts for over 60%.

You are permitted to work on your project outside of lesson time, including homework. Defold is free and can be installed on your own PC. However, your teacher must authenticate that the work you submit is yours, so they will want to see a substantial amount of it being produced in lessons too.

Before deciding to use Defold, you should complete several tutorials to learn how the engine works. There are plenty of tutorials and videos online. Craig 'n' Dave also produce a set of comprehensive tutorials that are suitable for A Level study and prepare you for undertaking an A Level project.

Examiner's advice

"Games offer a lot of opportunity to demonstrate high-level skills. Care must be taken that all the hard work is not being done by the underlying framework and that the candidate has built on top of it sufficiently."

An initial proposal

Before embarking on your project, it is a good idea to submit an initial proposal to your teacher; this will enable them to assess the scope and complexity of your project before you do too much work.

The project must be completed individually, not in a group. It is important to choose a project you will be interested in developing; this is a substantial piece of work - you need to enjoy it!

Your project proposal should include:

- A title.
- A brief overview of your idea.
- An outline of what you want to achieve as an outcome.

You do not need to submit your proposal in your final project. However, your teacher may decide to submit it to the examination board before you seek their guidance on scope, complexity and viability.

The role of your teacher

The Joint Council for Qualifications sets rigorous expectations on the completion of internally assessed work and clear guidelines for the role of the teachers assisting you.

Teachers **are** permitted to:

- Support you in choosing an appropriate project without giving you a specific idea. For example, your teacher could advise and help you choose from a list of your own ideas.
- Provide you with the mark scheme.
- Review your work and provide oral and written feedback at a general level.
- Allow you to redraft your work in response to this feedback.

Teachers are **not** permitted to:

- Provide you with writing frames or paragraph/section headings.
- Provide detailed, specific advice on how to improve drafts to meet the assessment criteria.*
- Give detailed feedback on errors and omissions.*
- Intervene to improve the presentation or content of your work.*
- Provisionally mark your work and then allow you to revise it.

**Unless they record the assistance and adjust marks accordingly.*

ANALYSIS

Outlining the genre of your project, identifying the player needs and exploring ideas to scope the success criteria.

In this section, you are discussing **what** game you are making.

10 marks

What to include

- An introduction to your project.
- Your target audience, an identified user and their role in your project.
- Detailed research into similar games.
- Features to be included in your game.
- Limitations of your development.
- Computational methods.
- Hardware and software requirements for development and deployment.
- Specific and measurable success criteria.

Project definition

You should start your project by providing a brief introduction to it. Set the scene so the examiner knows what your project is about; this is not detailed research but simply a brief overview limited to a few short paragraphs. It is not an essential section, but it will help give you the impetus to write more detailed research later. Getting started with the report is often the hardest part. Once you get going, it seems less daunting. It is important you do not use a template or simply copy the headings from another student. How you structure your writing is completely up to you. However, you should use a logical structure to make it easy for your teacher to mark and an examiner to moderate.

Things to consider:

- The history and context of your game.
- The aim of the game.
- Your intentions with the game.
- Your next steps, outlining how you will conduct further research.

When discussing the history and context of the game, you will need to find some reference material. You must write in your own words and reference your sources in a bibliography at the end of the project. You do not need to conform to a specific referencing standard.

A* TOP TIP

Do not forget to include a references or bibliography page in your report and keep a note of all your sources. You can only claim credit for original material.

An example of a project definition

In 1978, Tomohiro Nishikado created the iconic arcade game *Space Invaders*. It was the first fixed x-axis shooter in the shoot 'em up genre. The game was an immediate success and, by 1982, had made a profit of $450 million, making it the best-selling video game at the time.

History

The aim of the game is for a player controlling a spaceship to defeat continuous waves of descending alien craft and attempt to attain the highest score of the day. *Space Invaders* is considered one of the most influential games of all time, taking the video game industry from a novelty to a global industry. Even today, people like a game of *Space Invaders* due to its simplistic but addictive gameplay.

Aim

In this project, I aim to iterate upon the original design of *Space Invaders*, carefully retaining the best of the core game mechanics and introducing some new features.

Intentions

To do this, I am going to analyse the original game and a couple of similar games in detail. I will discuss these with a user from the intended target market to establish which mechanics to implement in my game.

Next steps

A* TOP TIP

Wikipedia can be a good place to start researching the history of your game, but do not simply copy and paste chunks of text. Instead, write in your own words.

Identifying suitable stakeholders

You need to identify who will be most likely to play your game. Avoid saying it is for everyone - you will have more to write about if you can target a specific audience. Preschool, junior school, teenagers and adults are examples of different audiences. Creating a game for preschool children with big buttons, primary colours, little text and a friendly fairy-tale narrative is quite different to creating a complex RPG for adults. Each audience has specific expectations.

Describe where your target audience is likely to play your game. Does it require the player to spend several hours at a PC over many days, months and years, or is it a simpler arcade game that can be played on a mobile phone in a bus shelter? Look at advertisements for games consoles; this will show you how different audience needs and play styles are taken into consideration.

Name a specific person from your target audience to be your "user". Explain their purpose in the development of the project. They are essential for:

- Giving you ideas for game mechanics.
- Testing your game as it is being developed, suggesting improvements and reviewing your development milestones.
- Beta-testing, evaluating and reviewing your game when it is complete.

The user must be a real person for them to give you feedback. A member of your family or a friend would be ideal. If necessary, they can be another student in your class. However, you may find you get more useful feedback from someone who is not studying computer science.

Examiner's advice

"This is more than identifying the stakeholders. Explain how they will play the game and what makes it suitable for the target audience."

ANALYSIS

Researching the problem in-depth

In this section of the analysis, you need to examine existing games that are like the game you are making - yes, that means playing some games! From this research, you will be able to make informed choices about which features you want to include in your own game.

If your game is an original idea, you may need to be more creative about which games to explore. Your game probably shares some features with existing games. For example, a tower defence game may share similarities with games like *Asteroids* and *Missile Command*, although it may not be immediately obvious. For example, both games require you to protect a ship from incoming objects.

Examining other similar games in the genre provides inspiration, ideas and talking points for discussion with your user. In the gaming industry, it is common for developers to brainstorm what they like and dislike about similar games and previous games in a series. Developers often want the player to feel like a game is recognisable but with enough new features to make it fresh and exciting. Sometimes these changes go down well with the audience - sometimes they do not.

The evolution of *Call of Duty* would make an interesting case study. When Respawn Entertainment conducted its research phase for *Titanfall*, the studio spent three months brainstorming ideas and deciding on the core mechanics and features of the game before even a single line of code was written. Developers listen to community feedback and think about where the industry is heading. The Battle Royale mode in *Fortnite* is an example of an iteration of a classic multiplayer mode that became an instant hit and was then copied into future versions of many other games.

Analysing existing games

To approach this section, you need to forensically analyse each aspect of the game you have chosen to explore. Take each object in the game and discuss what it looks like, how it moves, how it interacts with other objects and any associated sounds.

> **A* TOP TIP**
>
> The level of detail you include in your analysis will make a big difference to the mark you achieve. When examining the mechanics of other games, leave no stone unturned.

Look at the game more holistically too. For example, consider the scoring mechanics and how they are displayed to the player, how many lives a player has, whether they have a health bar, etc. Perhaps the player has an inventory or power-ups. What are they, how are they obtained, what are they worth and what do they do? Are there sound effects, multiple levels and game win/lose conditions? These are all examples of questions to answer.

Should you include screenshots?

Including some annotated screenshots in your work (with appropriate references) will help the examiner visualise what you are explaining.

How many games should you analyse?

It may be possible to capture everything you need from analysing one game in depth. However, exploring more than one game can make later sections of your report and justifications for your design decisions easier to write, so you should analyse two games as a minimum. If the first game you choose has a sequel or there are other titles like it, that would be ideal too.

There is no need to analyse games that are not like the one you want to make. The purpose of the analysis is to give you ideas about what to include in your own game and encourage you to think ahead.

> **A* TOP TIP**
>
> Analysing games that are similar but use different mechanics gives you plenty to write about when proposing your own game – for example, the concept of health and lives.

Stakeholder involvement

You may also choose to interview your user. There is no requirement to do this, but it is a good way to demonstrate how the stakeholders are involved in the process. You could capture this by writing up the key points from the discussion.

> ### Examiner's advice
>
> *"Interviews are not essential. Typing out interview transcripts is an unnecessary use of candidates' time. A summary of the interview's key points is sufficient."*

An approach to decomposition

One idea to help you structure your writing is to begin by taking a few different screenshots of the game you are researching and identify all the objects on the screenshot. Take each in turn and discuss:

- What it is (class).
- What properties it has (attributes).
- How it behaves (methods).

The use of subheadings will also help to structure your writing and make it easier to read.

An example of decomposition

Example 1: A vertical shooter

Objects to write about:

- Screen background
- Scoring and display
- UFO
- Invader
- Invader missile
- Player missile
- Shield
- Player ship
- Lives indicator

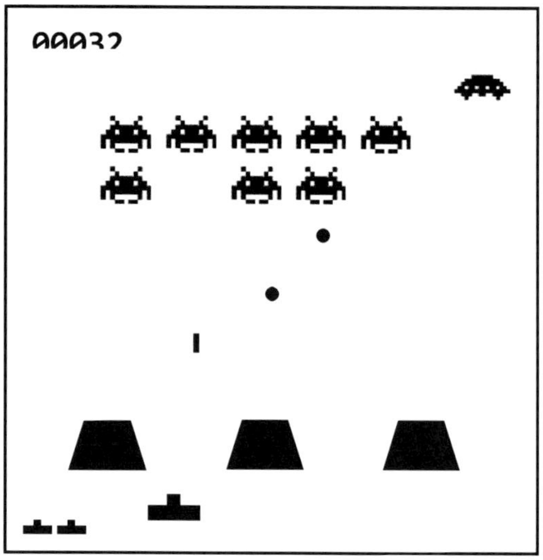

Example 2: A two-player tank game

Objects to write about:

- Background
- Scoring and display
- Walls
- Tanks
- Rockets
- Power-ups

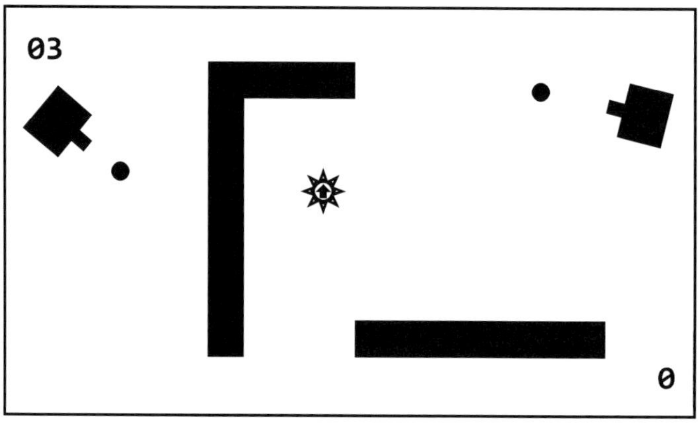

Identifying essential features of the proposed solution

Research is about problem decomposition and analysing existing games in detail. Once you have done that, you need to turn your attention to synthesis - that means considering all the ideas you have analysed to conclude what features your game will include.

Through your research, you will have uncovered different game mechanics. For example, a player may have a health bar, taking multiple hits before they die. They may have lives, where a single hit kills the player in an instant and they respawn. Alternatively, your game may use a combination of both - for example, a health bar that, once depleted, causes the player to lose a life before respawning. You should explain what your game design decisions are and, for top marks, justify them.

You may conclude that, given the number of enemies on the screen at any one time, having a simple one-hit-kill system would cause the player to lose a life too quickly and a health bar would provide the player with a more enjoyable experience.

Another example might be deciding where the player spawns. Typically, a player will spawn in a safe area where they are unlikely to be killed immediately, as that would be extremely frustrating for the player. The game designer may choose to kill all enemies before respawning the player or have a safe checkpoint to respawn the player, spawn them behind a shield or perhaps apply invincibility for a given number of seconds. These are all possibilities that change how the game is played.

> **A* TOP TIP**
> The difference between the top mark band and the 6- to 8-mark band is the word "justify". You must explain why you are including these features in your game.

Consider each of the game mechanics you researched in turn and decide how your game will work. Write about the mechanic and explain why you have made that choice. Do not forget, this will also include how the scoring system works, background graphics and sounds.

When you write this section, avoid using phrases such as, "I might." At this stage, it should be, "I will." That does not mean you cannot change your mind later - but be decisive.

Stakeholder involvement

It is essential to include a discussion with your stakeholders. You need evidence that they have been fully involved in the analysis stage. Your target market will bring many ideas to the table that you can consider and either accept or reject. Typically, some ideas will be easy to implement, and others will be extremely difficult. Explaining why a feature may be difficult for you to implement - and therefore, outside of the scope of the solution - makes for good justifications.

For example, your user could suggest adding a visual effect when your character runs along the ground, kicking up dirt. That may be easy to implement because Defold includes a particle engine you can use. You could implement it by spawning ten dirt objects and giving them a random trajectory and time to live. Equally, you may consider this feature unnecessary due to the level of abstraction you are aiming for. The decision can easily be justified either way but is a great example of a real game design process and how you can involve your stakeholder.

This diagram is a useful way to visualise what you are trying to achieve when identifying essential features:

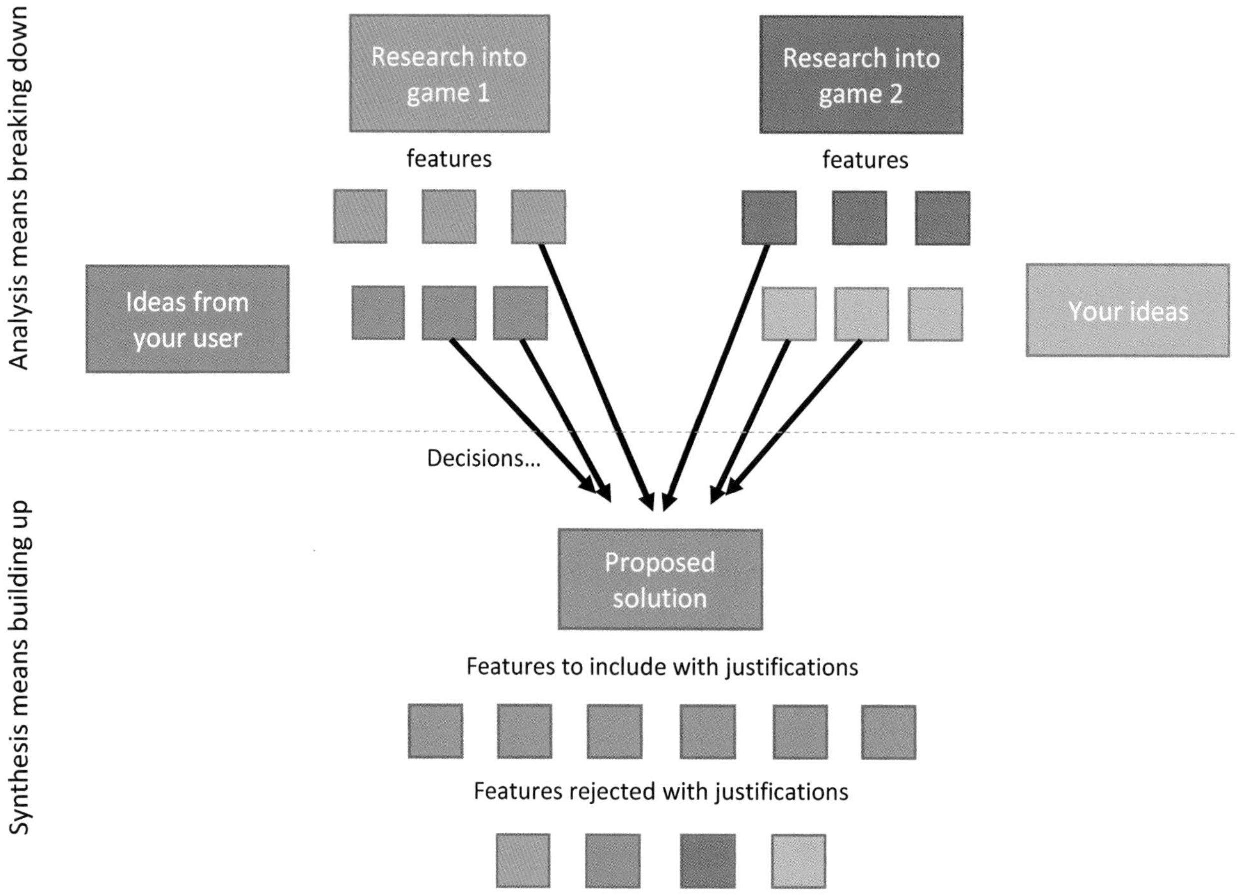

Identifying and explaining any limitations

It is better to have a smaller number of features implemented well than a large number unfinished. No development studio can ever do everything they want to do. They are limited by deadlines, money and programmer capacity. Be realistic about the time you have available. While it might be great to include a hundred levels with five types of player ship, 30 types of alien and 20 power-ups, you simply will not have time. Set yourself some limitations on the game you are making and describe them.

You may also be limited by your hardware and libraries. For example, dynamic lighting and shadow casting might be desirable but unachievable. You may have to simulate the input and output of your target device during development, especially if you are targeting the tablet, mobile or console market. For example, replacing analogue stick input with keyboard inputs or touchscreen tap with mouse clicks. These are all examples of limitations you could include in this section.

Computational methods

In many other types of projects, this section would be an opportunity to briefly explain why the problem can be solved by a computer. Problems that have identifiable inputs, algorithmic processes and outputs lend themselves to computation. With computer games, we need to approach this section of the report differently because, by their very nature, computer games are entertainment problems solved by a computer. It is useful to consider the computational methods and explain how they can be applied to the game you are making.

Aim to write a short paragraph about each of the computational methods described below.

Thinking abstractly

Abstraction is about identifying necessary and unnecessary details. You have already begun this process when considering your game mechanics and justifying the essential features of your solution. Here, you could describe what sprites (graphics), symbols and icons you need and why they might have a certain style to match your target market. You might also explain to what extent your game is a simulation of real life and why it might not need to be.

For example, you could explain that your player ship has a cone shape with boxes representing thrusters on either side. This sprite looks like rockets we have sent into space and is typical of the graphics seen in similar games, so the player will easily recognise the ship. However, because the game is intended to be an 8-bit retro game, there is no requirement for detailed graphics and textures.

You may describe a player's attributes being illustrated with simple icons on the screen. For example, a heart for health, a sword for strength and a shield for armour.

A* TOP TIP

It is important that this does not become a written account of the theory from component 2 of the course. You must apply the principles of what you have learned to your project.

Thinking ahead

Briefly describe what game worlds (output screens) you will have. For example, you might have a menu screen, a controls screen, a lore screen, a game over screen and a high-score table screen.

Then describe what your input mechanisms will be. For example, using W for up, S for down, A for left, D for right and Space to fire. Explain why you have chosen this mechanic - perhaps because it matches current gaming expectations.

Thinking procedurally and logically

Identify the core coded routines you will need. For example, moving the player, moving the enemies, players firing, enemies firing and collisions between players and enemies.

Thinking concurrently

Identify what aspects of the game logic can happen simultaneously. A good example is describing how sound and input will work concurrently with the game logic and screen rendering. It is possible to have sound effects playing at the same time as background music and user inputs using multi-channel sound. In Defold, the code for updating objects in the game may seem to be executing simultaneously.

Specifying hardware and software requirements

You need to discuss the hardware and software requirements for both development and deployment.

- State that you will be using the Defold IDE and Lua to make your game.
- State which operating system are you using - e.g., Windows, macOS or Linux.
- State the hardware required:
  - The Defold editor requires 4GB of RAM, with 6GB recommended for larger projects.
  - Defold uses OpenGL ES 2.0 for graphics rendering.
- Justify why Defold is a good engine for game development. Think about some of the great properties of Defold. These might include but are not limited to:
  - As a high-level language, Lua is quick to learn and easy to debug.
  - Wide variety of prebuilt assets including camera, tile sets and support for GUI interfaces.
  - Handling multitasking event processing - e.g., inputs, game logic and sound happening at the same time.
  - Handling the graphics card to ensure fast rendering and execution.
  - Automatic object pooling for performance and ease of coding.
  - Use of factories to create instances of game objects.
  - Encapsulation, message passing and easy-to-use object hierarchy.
  - Support for a wide range of deployment platforms - e.g., Apple App Store, Google Play Store, HTML5 and Java bytecode.

Avoid simply copying this list – you will gain no credit for that. Instead, think about how these could apply to your game and use specific examples.

The Defold SDK can be used to write extensions using additional C, C++, Objective-C, Java and JavaScript code. OpenGL ES SL shader language is used to write vertex and fragment shaders. However, you are very unlikely to be doing this in your project. Instead, you may use some third-party extensions such as Tiled, Defcon, Photoshop GUI Exporter and Polygon Editor, to name a few.

Defold also requires an executable run-time environment. Although you are writing your source code in Lua, it is compiled to Java bytecode to execute on your computer. Therefore, you will also need the Java virtual machine installed to run your game in a test environment on your PC.

> **A* TOP TIP**
> The deployment environment can often be different to the development environment. Games are developed on a PC using an SDK and ported to consoles and mobile devices.

It is also appropriate to state the input hardware required for your game. It is almost certain you will be developing your game on a PC and using a mouse and keyboard as your input mechanism. If your game is deployed to an alternative target platform, there is scope to use touch and controller inputs. Analogue inputs would allow the player to have greater control of their character, for example. It is not essential to include these in your actual game, but they are worthwhile considerations.

Examiner's advice

"It is recognised that some projects lend themselves more to discussion of hardware and software requirements. As such, some candidates will have little to write on this aspect."

Identifying and justifying measurable success criteria

In the concluding section of the analysis, you are summarising what you intend to achieve. It is important your criteria are specific, measurable and numbered for easy identification.

The success criteria serve three purposes:

1. An agreement about the scope of the solution - exactly what will be included in the game.
2. A framework to test the solution against.
3. A reference for the evaluation.

Statements such as "must be easy to use" are too subjective. For it to be a proper success criterion, you need to detail how it would be achieved rather than writing broad statements.

Examiner's advice

"Where candidates only have vague objectives like, "My game must be fun to play," they tend to not only drop marks in the analysis but also later in the project. Time spent on good-quality, measurable objectives pays dividends further down the line, as they form the backbone of strong testing and evaluation sections."

Analysts consider *volumetrics*, which means "how many and how often." Using numbers makes your objectives specific and easily measurable. For example, the player will have three lives; there will be four levels, six different enemies, two power-ups, etc.

There is no need to state what you will not include in your game. You considered this in the limitations section. The success criteria are a simplistic reference point for the rest of the project.

You should briefly justify each of your choices. You are not completely rewriting the features of the proposed solution section but summarising the key reason for including the feature in the scope.

A good approach is to number each of your criteria so you can use the same number system later when discussing them in the testing and evaluation section. Aim for between 12 and 30 criteria. Too few, and you probably do not have sufficient scope and complexity for an A Level project. Too many, and you risk giving yourself too much work to do in the time available.

The example below is presented in a table, simply to illustrate the numbering of the criteria and how they can be justified more easily. There is no requirement for you to present your criteria in this way.

An example of success criteria for *Space Invaders*

No.	Criteria	Justification
1	Display a menu screen to the player, including options to play the game and change sound settings.	The player needs to be ready to play the game. Displaying a menu will enable the player to choose when to start. The player can also change some of the settings to make the game more enjoyable.
2	Display the number of lives a player has.	The player needs to know how many lives they have left before the game is over. Icons are an effective, space-efficient way to achieve this.
3	Display the score.	The player needs to know how well they are doing.
4	Allow the player to move left and right and fire.	Movement should challenge the player, so it should take approximately three seconds to move from one side of the screen to another. The player cannot leave the screen. To make the game more challenging, the player can only fire one missile at a time.
5	Score points for shooting an alien - e.g., octopus alien, 10 points; squid alien, 20 points; crab alien, 50 points; UFO, random number of points between 100 and 300 in multiples of 50.	The player should be encouraged to attempt to shoot the UFO; this will add more challenge to achieving a high score in the game.
6	Start the player with three lives.	Makes the game challenging without being too difficult. The player will be able to play the game for a reasonable amount of time per session.
7	Display 55 aliens in 11 rows.	Prevents the player from depleting the aliens too quickly.

8	Move the aliens as a group from right to left until they reach the edge of the screen and then reverse their direction.	The aliens move slowly and gain speed as more are shot; this makes the game more challenging.
9	Randomly display a UFO at the top of the screen, moving either left to right or right to left until it leaves the screen.	Allows the player to gain more points quickly and makes the game more interesting.
10	Only display a UFO if more than eight aliens are alive.	Prevents the player from keeping one alien alive for longer to make the UFO easier to hit.
11	The bottom alien in any column can fire back randomly.	Makes the game more unpredictable and harder to play. However, it would seem odd if aliens shot through each other.
12	Up to 20 alien missiles will be on-screen at any one time.	Balances challenge with the impact of having to update many objects at once on the frame rate.
13	There will be two types of alien missile.	Increases the graphical appeal to the game.
14	Background music and sound effects.	The music will speed up as the aliens are shot to increase tension. Sound effects will make the game more appealing.

Examiner's advice

"The requirements and success criteria are part of the key to a good project. An ideal set of requirements should be detailed enough to pass onto a third party to design the system."

SECTION		DO's		DON'Ts
Project definition	1	Set the scene for the examiner.	☐	Assume the examiner will have played games in your chosen genre.
	2	State your intentions and next steps for research.	☐	
Identifying suitable stakeholders	3	Identify the target market for your game and use the PEGI system to inform your choices.	☐	Be both the developer and player of your game. Make sure you have someone else representing the target market to give you objective feedback.
	4	Involve a representative from your stakeholders throughout your project using a RAD approach to development.	☐	
Research	5	Provide detailed research into existing games like the one you are making.	☐	Rely on your own input only for the research.
	6	Include details about all the objects in the games and their methods.	☐	Undertake a game that is like someone else's in your class.
	7	Include a summary of the discussion with a stakeholder.	☐	Write up interviews as a Q&A session.
	8	Include a references or bibliography at the end of your project report.	☐	Forget you need a bibliography.
Features of the proposed solution	9	Identify the features you are going to include in your game.	☐	Attempt to make a game that is too complex in the time allowed.
	10	Identify any limitations of your proposed development.	☐	Settle for a simplistic game that is not going to have some challenges you can discuss later.
	11	Be realistic about what can be achieved in the time allowed.	☐	
Computational methods	12	Explain how you will make use of abstraction, thinking ahead, thinking logically and thinking concurrently.	☐	Explain the theory of computational methods from unit 2.
Hardware and software requirements	13	Specify the hardware requirements for the target platform, including input devices.	☐	Forget there are requirements for both development and deployment.
	14	Specify the software requirements for your development including the operating system.	☐	Simply identify the programming language you are using without justification.
	15	Identify any additional utilities or libraries that will be required to make your game.	☐	
Success criteria	16	Specify the measurable requirements for the game.	☐	State vague subjective criteria that are difficult to measure.
	17	Justify why each requirement is necessary.	☐	

DESIGN

The plan for your development.

In this section, you are discussing **how** you are **going** to solve the problem.

15 marks.

What to include

- A structure diagram illustrating the problem decomposition.
- Explanation of all the game objects.
- Algorithms in pseudocode for the methods in the scripts.
- Usability features.
- Data structures to be used.
- Input validation.
- Test data to be used during the development of the coded solution.
- Test data to be used post-development.

Breaking the problem down systematically

This section of your report explains the structure of your intended solution. In the analysis section, you explored other people's work and described your intentions; this was about *what* you were going to do. In the design section, you are writing about *how* you are going to realise these intentions.

Start with a structure diagram, which will illustrate the subroutines you intend to develop. Below is an example of a structure diagram for a typical arcade shooter.

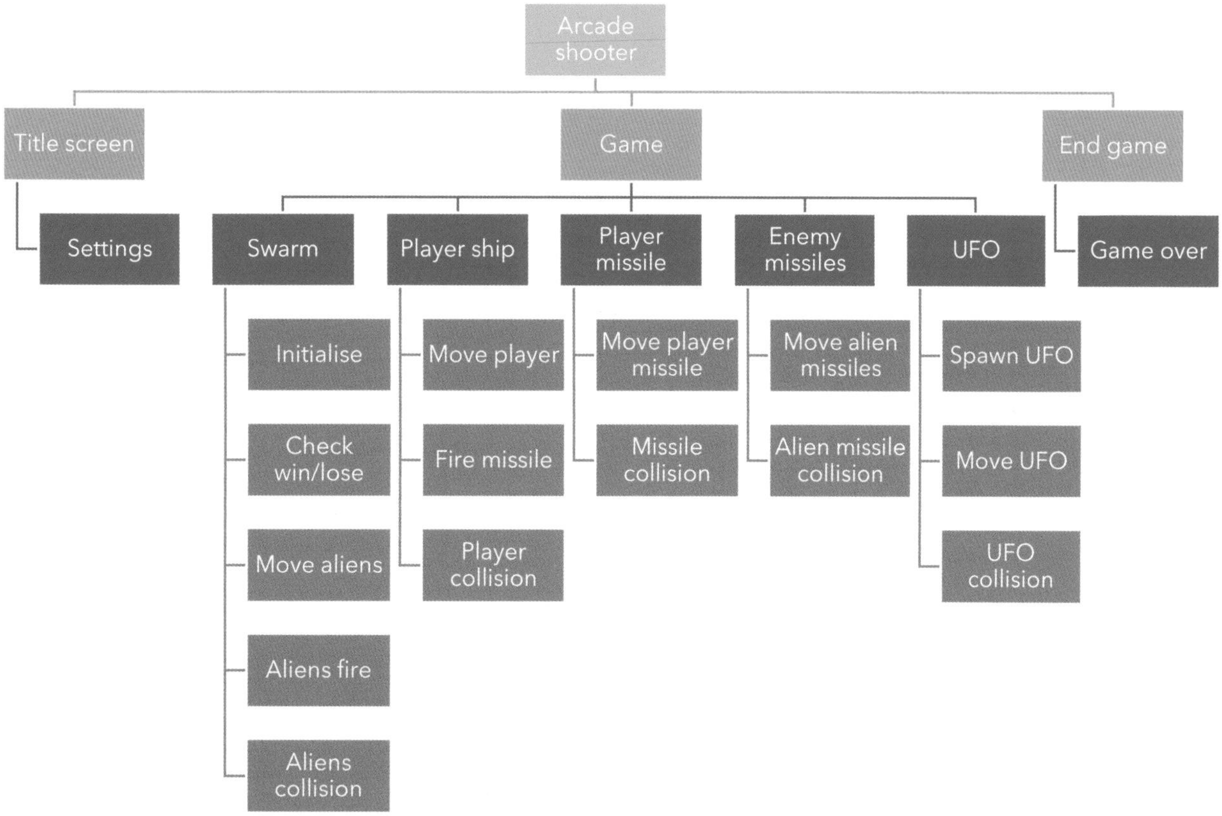

DESIGN

> You need to balance the level of detail you decide to include on your structure diagram. If it does not fit on the page or is unreadable, you have included too much detail.
>
> A* TOP TIP

Notice how the number of boxes underneath the ones above increase; this shows the problem being broken down into increasingly smaller parts. There is no right answer to producing this diagram - it depends on how you visualise the game you are going to make.

The top (yellow) box is the name of your game, while the boxes underneath the title (green) are the key interface screens the user will see. Below these are the main game objects (blue), followed by the actions those objects can take (orange). Later, these will be routines written in scripts.

The colours are not important. Choose your own style, providing it is easy to read. Using SmartArt hierarchy objects in your word processing application is acceptable. Avoid using 3D shapes, as these will be difficult to read and do not follow industry conventions.

Notice we have not included aspects of the game that Defold automatically handles like rendering the screen. There is no need to include parts you will not develop; this is an overview of *your* development.

This diagram becomes a handy reference for the rest of your project because the examiner should be able to follow each box to later sections of your report - e.g., algorithms, coded solution and testing.

> Although it is possible to combine the design and code sections of your report in an iterative way, make sure your work still meets all the mark scheme criteria for design.
>
> A* TOP TIP

Defining the structure of the solution to be developed

Think about how your structure diagram can now be applied to a Defold development. Create a list of the assets and components required to illustrate the skeleton design of your game as it would appear in the outline panel. Remember, interfaces require collection proxies and objects spawned dynamically will require a factory. The objects created by a factory are often assets that are not listed in the outline, but you should still include them to show the structure of your solution.

Part of the list of assets is shown below. Colour is used to illustrate how it maps to the structure diagram.

- Arcade shooter
  - Project settings
  - Input bindings
- Collection: main
  - Game object: controller
  - Collection proxy: title screen
  - Collection proxy: game
  - Collection proxy: end game
- Collection: title
  - GUI object: title screen
  - GUI script: title screen
- Collection: game
  - Game object: player missile
    - Collision object: player missile
    - Script: player missile
    - Sprite: player missile
  - Game object: player ship
    - Collision object: player ship
    - Script: player ship
    - Sprite: player ship
  - Game object: swarm
    - Factory: aliens
      - Game object: alien
        - Collision object: alien
        - Particle FX: explosion
        - Sprite: alien
    - Script: swarm
  - Collection: end game
    - GUI object: game over screen
    - GUI script: end game

Explaining the game objects

Now take each of the boxes in the structure diagram in turn. State which script will host the code being written and explain what happens in this part of the game.

An example of a paragraph for this section

Firing a missile

This routine will be in the on_update method of the player ship script. It handles a player being able to fire at the aliens.

A missile is spawned when the player presses Space. A missile can only be spawned if one is not already on the screen. It will start in the middle of the player ship. If it has a lower Z index than the ship, it will look like the missile is coming out of the ship as it moves because the ship will be drawn on top of the missile.

Explaining what happens in detail

This routine helps make the game more realistic. The initial speed of the missile will be set so it takes some time to hit a target, making the game more challenging.

Justification

It is important to remember the design section is not as much about *what* you are going to do (this was discussed in the analysis) but more about *how* you are going to do it. If you get this section right, you should be able to write basic pseudocode from it in the next section of your report.

For top marks, you will need to justify your design decisions. These are not justifications of the inclusion of features – you did this in the analysis section. You are justifying how these features will be implemented. For example, when discussing how the aliens move down the screen:

The aliens need to move together as a group when one reaches the edge of the screen. Instead of each alien having its own script and using message passing to tell the other aliens to move down, a swarm game object can be used to control all the aliens at the same time. Storing the aliens in a table data structure will allow for easy iteration over all the aliens.

Justification

DESIGN

Examiner's advice

"Candidates who opt to take an object-oriented approach tend to fare especially well in the design section, having a clear idea as to how their project can be decomposed."

Algorithms

This section of your report is not the actual code but, instead, the algorithms you intend to write. It is a decomposition of the actions and scripts you identified in the systems diagram and a list of components (coloured orange).

Although you can use flowcharts, they get unwieldy very quickly when algorithms become more complex and are time-consuming to produce. It is advised that you use pseudocode in this section.

Algorithms are represented with pseudocode so they can be interpreted by programmers, irrespective of the programming languages they are familiar with. Pseudocode, as the name suggests, is a false code or a representation of code that can be understood by most people.

The differences between algorithms, pseudocode and source code

Algorithm: A logical sequence of the actions of a process. A programmer implements an algorithm using source code. They then express it in a language-independent way using pseudocode.

Pseudocode: Has no defined syntax, so it cannot be compiled or interpreted by the computer. However, it is written in a way that makes it easy to produce real code for most languages.

Plain English	Pseudocode	Source code	Machine code
Describing your solution (the previous part of your report)	Proposed algorithms for procedures/functions/methods (this part of your report)	The real programming code for your game (developing a coded solution)	Binary the computer executes

There is no requirement to use the examination board reference language. These are for writing examination questions only.

At this stage, you might feel you do not have the confidence to write your algorithms. Perhaps you're not entirely sure what you are going to do - in which case, your analysis and the first part of your project may be weak - or you're not sure how to write the code because of insufficient experience with Defold and Lua. If you hit a brick wall here, go back and make sure you have been decisive about the mechanics of your game in the previous section.

Once you have done that, remember - pseudocode is not real code. Have a go at identifying the logical steps, invent commands as you need to and use variables as you write the commands.

Basic building blocks of pseudocode

In Defold development, each script has several subroutines:

- **Init:** A constructor - code executes here when the object spawns.
- **Update:** Code to move objects.
- **On_input:** Code to respond to inputs.
- **On_message:** Code to send and receive messages to other objects.

Think about the scripts you identified. Using pseudocode, state what will happen in each of these subroutines for each game object.

You should use indenting with pseudocode, just like with real code.

It may not be obvious why you have approached a specific routine in the way you have. There are often hundreds of different ways to write an algorithm, each delivering the same output. Therefore, you should justify your approach where appropriate.

Let us take another look at the fire missile routine. Our pseudocode becomes:

Pseudocode	Justification
`Key Trigger: [space] or [Enter] then action_id = fire` `if action_id = fire then`	Space and Enter will both have key bindings set to the fire action so the player has a choice of input mechanisms.
`if missile_alive = false then`	Missile_alive is a Boolean because only one missile can be on the screen at a time.

`player = get_position(player_object)`
`missile = get_position(missile_object)`
`missile.x = player.x`
`missile.y = player.y`
`set_position(missile)`
	The missile needs to spawn at the same position as the player ship.

You should have a pseudocode routine for each major algorithm in your game. There is no need to design trivial algorithms used for pressing buttons on GUIs. For example, you may have an interface where the user clicks a button to play the game. The actual code to achieve this could be:

```
if action.pressed and GUI.pick_node(GUI.get_node("play"), action.x, action.y) then
    msg.post("main:/controller", "play_game")

end
```

It is not necessary to include these minor algorithms. Equally, if you are likely to have many repeating code elements, it would be appropriate to show these only once - but remember, if this is the case, you would be better off using a subroutine anyway.

A* TOP TIP

Remember, justifications are the key to achieving the highest grade. Justify why you need the algorithms you have designed.

It is not essential to justify every line of code, as shown in the example. It is acceptable to justify blocks of code instead. For example, if you decide to implement a linear search, hashing or a sorting algorithm, it would be acceptable to justify the algorithm itself and why alternatives are not suitable rather than justifying individual lines of code.

You will know you have achieved a good report if the examiner can "follow the thread" of small aspects of your project, from the initial research through to success criteria and design. Make sure they can see the algorithms and understand how they were coded, tested and evaluated. Everything needs to be coherent and easy to follow throughout your project report.

Examiner's advice

"Reverse-engineered code is given no credit."

Describing usability features included in the solution

Interfaces

Computer games typically have three main interfaces; a screen presented when the game has loaded, a screen where the game is played and an after-game screen. However, there could be many more screens too. This section of your report should illustrate the proposed screen designs and input mechanisms, explaining how they make the game easy to understand and play for the user.

Consider a typical first-person shooter game. They usually have a head-up display (HUD), on-screen markers (e.g., grenade proximity), ammo indicators, killstreak indicators, etc. These are all part of the user interface, and their inclusion (or exclusion) should be justified. It is a good idea to get user feedback on these designs and include it in this section of your report.

For example, in *Call of Duty: Modern Warfare (2019)*, a decision was initially taken to remove the HUD to make the game feel more realistic and less like an arcade game. However, after community feedback, the HUD was included in the final build, although red markers indicating where players are shooting from - a feature of previous games - was still removed and placed on a compass instead. A frequent complaint in previous games in the franchise was that enemy footsteps were too quiet, so the volume was significantly increased. These are all part of the usability considerations.

DESIGN

An example of a screen design for an arcade shooter:

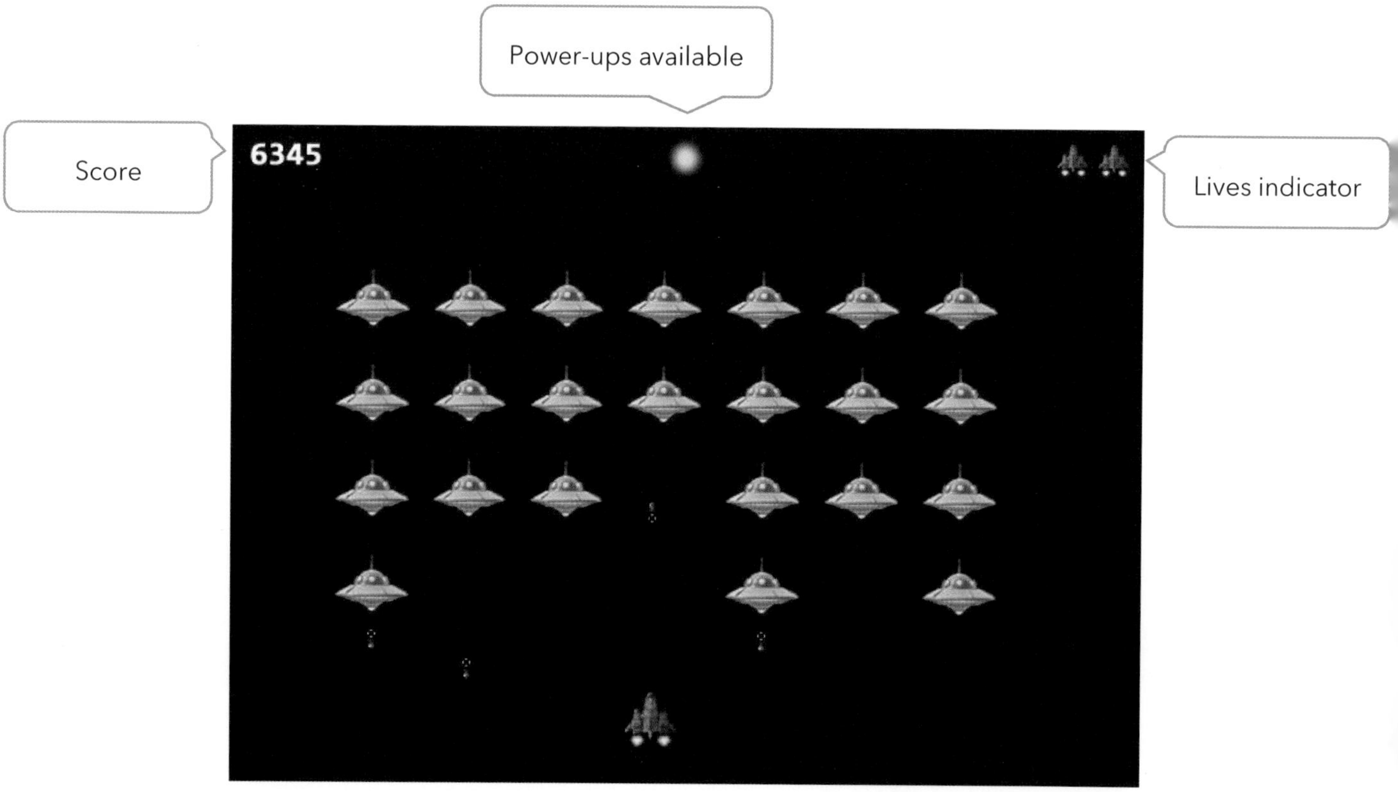

Sketch your proposed interfaces and label the considerations. You can hand-draw this concept art and scan it into your document, compose the picture from several graphical elements such as shapes and icons found in many office programs or use a graphics program such as Photoshop, GIMP or even Paint. These should be proposed screen designs and not actual screenshots from your game.

> **A* TOP TIP**
> At the design stage, you produce concept art, not screenshots from the final product. It is also acceptable to create a non-working prototype to illustrate your design.

At this stage, there are probably very few things about the interface you have not already discussed in previous sections of your report; this is the final opportunity to discuss anything that is not obvious. For example, you may decide to use an animation to show the player ship tilting left and right when it is moving. You should explain these visual indicators and why they are a feature of your game.

If you are using icons in your game – for example, to represent different power-ups – these should each be drawn and explained. You should also consider colour-blind players. What will you do to your interface to ensure these players are not disadvantaged? Having green and red markers can often be changed to orange and blue in the options, for example; this is certainly not a requirement for your project, but this kind of thinking about the target market can attract the highest marks.

Player experience

You could explain how your game will increase in difficulty and help the player. Many modern games walk the player through a tutorial mission with short, simple objectives to familiarise them with the controls and actions they can take.

There is no requirement to do this in your game, as it is likely to be very time-consuming to implement. In simplistic ways, you may consider how you help your player have a good experience – for example, spawning in a place where they cannot instantly die.

> **A* TOP TIP**
> Discussing the player experience is not essential, but it does provide you with plenty of opportunity to justify your design decisions.

Your choice of input mechanism is intended to make the game easier or harder to play. For example, a power-up could grant the player rapid fire for a limited time. You could allow the player to hold down the fire key or ensure they release the key before pressing it again. There is no correct choice here; it depends on what experience you want the player to have.

Other considerations you may discuss in this section include accessibility, believability and forgiveness in the collision detection. For example, car racing games are heavily abstracted. The non-player character (NPC) cars change their speed according to the player; this prevents them getting too far ahead, making it impossible for the player to catch up, and adds enjoyment at the expense of realism. Hitboxes in arcade shooters are usually generous so a player does not feel cheated. Situations where the player dies and feels it should not have happened do not make for a good experience. You can discuss all these considerations in this section.

If you feel you are at risk of repeating what you have written in previous sections, simply add some cross-references instead. For example, "Playability considerations were discussed in the features of the proposed solution section on page 20."

Identifying the data structures and validation

Now that you have written your algorithms, you should be able to identify all the constants, variables, data structures and files you need. Although Lua is not object-oriented, Defold developments share many of the same paradigm characteristics, so you should include class diagrams for your objects.

Class diagrams

There are three rectangular sections to each class diagram.

Attributes are the variables and constants.

These are often used with the "self" table structure in Defold. State what they hold with justifications using annotations.

Methods are the subroutines (init, update, on_input and on_message), plus any user-defined functions you make.

You will have several small class diagrams - most likely one for each object in your game.

Name of the class
Attributes
Methods

Remember, to achieve the top mark band, you need to justify your choices. For example, you might be using prehashing to improve performance or user-defined functions to eliminate repeated code. If you are using a table data structure, perhaps this is because you want to iterate through the structure with a loop or maybe because it is dynamic and items can easily be added and removed.

Boolean data types have two states, making them an ideal choice for when situations need to be stored as true or false, on or off. In modern developments, programmers often avoid using a Boolean so a third and fourth state can be introduced later if a future iteration of the project requires it.

Remember, if your program's values do not change, using constants is more efficient, as the compiler can use immediate instead of relative addressing, speeding up the execution of your program - critical in game development. Although Lua does not support constants with a keyword, "hard-coding" values to a variable and not changing them achieves the same outcome during compilation.

In addition to the classic data structures, you should consider the need for higher-order data structures such as graphs and trees.

An example class diagram

Each variable, constant and attribute should be identified. Although you do not declare the data type in Lua, for the purposes of the project report and demonstrating to the examiner that you understand it, you should.

A table is a useful way to do this.

Alien

`pos.x: integer`
`pos.y: integer`
`can_fire: Boolean`

`Init(self)`
`Update(self, dt)`
`On_input(self, action)`
`On_message(self, message)`

An example of a variable table with justifications

Variable	Data type	Purpose, justification and validation
`player.x` `player.y`	Integer	Stores the horizontal and vertical position of the player. Will be converted to a Vector3 to allow another vector to be applied and change the position.
`Missile_alive`	Boolean	Stores whether the player has fired a missile and whether it is alive to prevent more than one missile being fired. A Boolean has two states, so "true" can identify that a player has fired.
`dt`	Real	The delta time - the time difference between the last frame and the current frame. Multiplied by the movement vector, this will ensure a consistent movement speed across different processors.

There will be many more variables than those presented in the example above. Several smaller tables for each of the game objects would make your work easier to follow. In addition to the class attributes, you may have global or other local variables - remember to include those too.

> It may seem odd to justify your variables, especially if you name them appropriately. However, justifications are a key requirement of achieving marks in the top mark band.
>
> A* TOP TIP

Developers spend hours looking for minor savings in memory and processing. Not only is memory and clock speed a limiting factor but also, increasing the amount of code to process in the game logic lowers the frame rate. An art of game design is to find every optimisation you can. Carefully justifying why variables and routines are needed can be very important.

Files

If your game uses external files, it is important to illustrate the structure of how the data is being stored because it will be an abstraction - i.e., the relationship between the data and the program will not be immediately obvious.

For example, consider the data file to the right, named "level1.txt". It is not obvious what the values represent. What is the number 1050? Why is it needed? Where does one record end and another one start?

```
5000
1
2
1300
200
3
1050
1
3
-50
200
```

Using structured files like JSON can help alleviate this. However, if you are using files to load and save data, you should describe one record of the structure.

An example of an annotated file

Level1.txt	
5000 1 2 1300 200 3	The spawn time in milliseconds. The type of alien: 1-4. The waypoint pattern to follow. 2 is down the screen from top to bottom. The x spawn point. The y spawn point. The health of the alien.
5500 1 2 1300 200 3	The next record...

DESIGN

Encoding

Note that we identified the alien type with a number from 1 to 4. Using values to represent types of components is common in game design. For example, in a breakout game, a red brick might be represented with a 1, a yellow brick with a 2, a green brick with a 3, a two-hit brick with a 4 and an indestructible brick with a 5. Level data is often represented like this too – e.g., a wall might be 1, a key might be 2, etc. In Defold, you may be using a tile source and tile map for this purpose. You must explain all the encoding you are using so it is obvious what the values in the code represent.

Including a screenshot of any tile sources you are using is helpful to understand the encoding.

A* TOP TIP

Validation

Validation in games is often different to other computer systems. The user rarely has enough freedom to generate invalid inputs unless you are creating an adventure game that has a command-line input option. Instead, the user typically has a series of menu choices to select from or input keys to press.

However, there are situations where an input could result in an invalid action; this will need to be trapped in the code. A good example is player movement. You may prevent the player character leaving the screen by checking the x position variable and only changing it if the character will not leave the screen; this is an example of validation that you could discuss. Equally, you may prevent this action by ensuring a level is surrounded by walls, also preventing the player from leaving the screen.

In this section, discuss and justify the potential situations that require validation checks. You can identify them in your algorithms because they will be selection statements such as IF against player-controlled variables. If applicable, you can also state which menus you have, why you chose this input mechanism and what the options are.

Examiner's advice

"At the top end, there should be a clear decomposition of the problem into key elements and algorithms to match each element."

Identifying test data to be used during iterative development

At this point, it is worth reflecting on your systems diagram that you started this section with and the code you are going to write, which you stated in the algorithms section. From this, identify six to ten key milestones. You will use these later in the coded solution. For example:

1. Main interfaces
2. Move the player
3. Spawn the aliens
4. Move the aliens
5. Fire at the aliens, collision detection and score
6. Aliens fire back
7. Losing lives and the game
8. Starting new levels

For each of these key milestones, identify the test conditions you will need for that milestone and present them in a table.

A development test example

Milestone 2: Move the player		
Test number	**What is being tested and inputs**	**Expected output**
1	The player spawns on the screen.	The player sprite appears at the bottom-left area of the screen.
2	The player can move left with A and right with D.	The player moves left and right at a reasonable speed but cannot leave the screen.
3	An animation is played when the player moves.	The ship sprite changes to bank left and right and idle when no key is pressed.

Identifying further data to be used post-development

This section is about how you will test that your game is balanced and fun. In large multiplayer developments, designers need to stress-test their game under the heavy server loads that are expected during the game's initial launch period. They will also want to heavily test the new player experience to check that the rate of progression is appropriate. As you playtest your game during development, it will become easier for you to play. One of the major problems in game design is that the studio becomes too good at the game they are making and risk making it too hard for a new player; this is one reason why beta testing is a good idea.

> **A* TOP TIP**
> Remember to justify the tests you are going to perform later to achieve top marks.

There will undoubtedly be balance issues - for example, between weapons. Alternatively, some levels might be too easy or too hard. It is difficult to test this until the game is nearly complete. You will not be testing your game to the same extent. Instead, you will compare your solution to the success criteria you set in the analysis section; this is an opportunity to include those tests that are less measurable and more about the feel of the game. You may have omitted these in the requirements specification because they are subjective. For example, the game should be fun - how will you test and measure this? Perhaps you could conduct a beta test with a small number of players and get their feedback.

A post-development test example

Post-development test	Testing to be performed post-development	Justification
The game increases in difficulty as it is played.	The aliens start further down the screen with each wave. The aliens move faster with each wave. The average player can complete at least two waves successfully.	For the game to be fun, it needs to be challenging but allow the player enough time to play the game before dying.

SECTION		DO's		DON'Ts
Structure of the game	18	Provide an overview of the structure of your game using a diagram to illustrate breaking the problem down into smaller parts.	☐	Be concerned about using a JSP/UML standard.
Breaking the problem down systematically	19	Provide evidence of problem decomposition by explaining each component of your game.	☐	Reverse engineer your completed program. Your code will likely deviate from these initial design ideas. Include screen shots from your finished program. Spend too much time on graphics and colourful illustrations.
	20	Include sketches of interface designs.	☐	
	21	Explain the input validation that will be necessary.	☐	
	22	Consider the usability features of your program and expected UI conventions.	☐	
	23	Justify your approaches to all the above.	☐	
Algorithms	24	Provide a set of language independent algorithms to describe each of the subroutines and methods.	☐	Use flowcharts, they are too cumbersome for large problems.
	25	Use your own pseudocode standard if you need to use commands you are not familiar with.	☐	Provide code or reverse engineered code as an algorithm.
Data structures	26	Provide class diagrams if you are taking an object-oriented approach.	☐	Forget to include descriptions of any encoding. Forget to include a file structure reference.
	27	Explain and justify the variables and data structures that you will be using.	☐	
	28	Show the file format and encoding if you are using files or tile sources.	☐	
Test data for development	29	Identify 6-10 milestones for the development.	☐	Do this retrospectively. Test data should be drawn up in advance of development. Forget that good testing includes a variety of situations for each object.
	30	Identify the tests that need to be performed for each milestone before it can be considered complete.	☐	
Test data for post-development	31	Identify and justify testing that needs to be performed when all the modules have been developed.	☐	Avoid issues where your program fails. These are good to talk about even if they are not resolved. Forget that post development includes integration, alpha and beta testing.
	32	Identify data that is designed to test the robustness of the game; good testing should attempt to break the program.	☐	

DEVELOPING A CODED SOLUTION

The iterative development process.

In this section, you are discussing **how** you have made a **solution** to the problem.

15 marks	Coded solution
10 marks	Testing to inform development

What to include

- Evidence of developing each milestone.
- Explanations of what you did and why.
- Annotated code with suitably named variables and routines.
- Evidence of input validation.
- Review of each milestone.

An agile approach to development

At the end of the design section, you identified six to ten key milestones. In this section, you need to provide evidence of developing each of those milestones. The development must be an iterative process. That means you cannot just provide a code listing of your finished product. Instead, you must document the story of how the development evolved as it was being coded.

It is expected that your development will change from your initial design ideas. Rarely do games become exactly what was initially proposed. When you do change your mind, you do not need to go back and change your analysis and design. Instead, document your changes and the reasons behind them in this section of your report. If the change is so fundamental that the design no longer resembles the development, you may want to go back and make your report more coherent, but this should rarely be necessary unless your analysis was very weak.

In this section of your report, you will be including parts of your code. If it is practical to do so, it is helpful to include a full code listing in an appendix at the end of your project. In this section, you will provide only parts of the code that are relevant to each milestone.

When developing a milestone, you will frequently need to return to previous aspects of the code to make changes or add new routines. Do not include code sections you have already included in your report previously - just the new parts.

Examiner's advice

"At the top end, candidates have clear and discrete iterations. Each iteration has stated objectives, which were tested and evaluated at the end of the iteration."

Documenting the milestones

For *each* milestone, include the following:

1. **Objective of the milestone:** In one or two sentences, describe what this milestone achieves.
2. **Code listing:** Provide a listing of the code for this milestone. Code must be commented with appropriate variable and data structure names.
3. **Explanation of the code:** Explain what the code section does and justify algorithms or approaches. It might not be immediately obvious to an examiner how the code works or why problems have been solved in the way they have. Remember, the examiner may not be familiar with the language you are using. If input validation is required, explain that too.
4. **Module testing:** Explain the tests you performed for this section of code and the outcome of those tests. You will likely be playing the game and tweaking the variables a lot to get the outcome you want. You should provide evidence of this process.
5. **User feedback:** Your user should tell you what they like and dislike about this aspect of the development so far, with ideas for future development. Your user must be an integral part of the iterative development process.
6. **Reflections:** As a result of playtesting and user feedback, discuss what needs to be changed.

A* TOP TIP

The very best projects tell the story of the development. You do not need to include commentary of resolving every single error, but you should explain the challenges you faced.

A* TOP TIP

Do not forget to justify the approaches you have taken in the explanation of the code – especially if they are different to your original design intentions.

Example of one milestone

Spawning the alien swarm and displaying them on the screen

Code I wrote to achieve this milestone:

```
function new_swarm(self)
-- spawn aliens
        self.swarm_table = {}
        self.speed = 100
        self.direction = 1
        local pos
        local alien_id

        -- set position of the alien on the screen
        for y = 500,290,-70 do
                for x = 100,550,70 do
                        pos = vmath.vector3(x,y,0)
                        alien_id = factory.create("#alien_factory", pos)

                        -- hold reference to alien
                        table.insert(self.swarm_table,alien_id)
                end
        end
end
```


Examiner's advice

"Care must be taken that code shown in screenshots is big enough and of a high enough resolution. Ideally, syntax highlighting should be preserved. It is the responsibility of candidates to ensure that their final PDF or printed copy is readable. Credit cannot be given for code that cannot be read."

Explanation of the code

Before writing this code, I created a new factory object that would create an instance of the alien class when called. Using this new object was preferable to manually creating each alien and placing them on the canvas, as it will allow me to change the number of aliens in a swarm and start a new level by initialising the aliens again very easily.

I wrote a user-defined function called "new_swarm" that will handle spawning a new wave of aliens. I did it this way instead of coding it within a method so I could call this subroutine every time I wanted a new wave to spawn.

A table data type is used to store all the aliens; this is required so I can iterate over all the aliens to change their vertical position when one hits the edge of the screen.

The speed of each alien is held in an attribute called "speed". I can change this to make the aliens move faster as the game progresses, increasing the difficulty.

Direction holds which way the aliens are moving, 1 for moving right or -1 for left; this makes it easier to change their x position, as it is an integer. The aliens start by moving right.

A nested loop positions each new alien on the screen. I can use the loop starting, ending and step values to avoid having additional variables or calculations. "Pos" is a vector data type holding the x and y position of each alien. The factory is called to spawn a new alien at the vector position; this returns a pointer to the alien. This pointer is stored in the table so it can be referenced later.

Module testing

I tested that the aliens appeared on the screen in their correct position. When I ran the program, four rows of seven aliens were shown in the middle of the screen. The horizontal spacing between the aliens looked a little too small, making the game too easy, so I increased the step from 70 to 75 in the loop.

Evidence

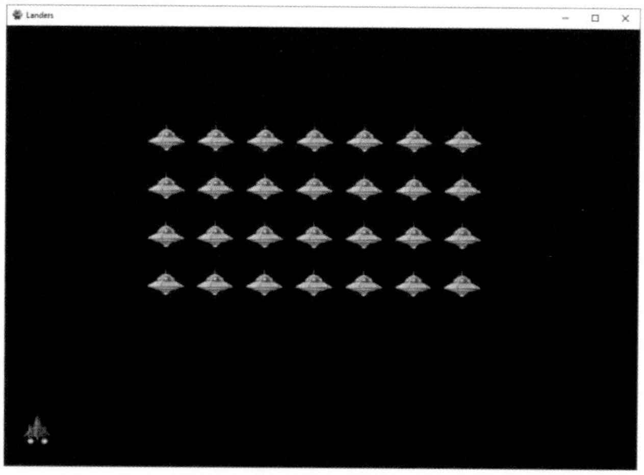

User feedback

My user thought that the number of aliens was probably too few to make the game challenging and that the vertical spacing between them was too large. They suggested the swarm should be larger but more compact. They liked the position of the aliens on the screen.

Reflections

Spawning aliens in the middle of the screen and not at the top left room for the UFO and score; it also makes it more challenging. I can easily make the changes my user is suggesting by reducing the loop step from -75 to -70, decreasing the loop starting value and increasing the ending value by multiples of 70. I originally intended the aliens to move in blocks rather than smoothly across the screen; this was achieved in the original game because the CPU was so slow it took a long time to update the position of each alien. However, the modern PC I am using updated the position too quickly. I tried introducing a loop to slow it down, but I realised this would execute at different speeds on different computers.

Instead, I tried using the delta time. Although it worked, it looked odd, so I changed my mind from the original requirements to include a smooth movement, which seemed much better visually. I may come back to this later to add an entry animation so the aliens fly in from the top of the screen before reaching their starting position; this would make the game visually interesting and more polished.

A* TOP TIP

It is expected that your coded solution will deviate from your design. There is no need to rewrite the design section – this gives you plenty to write about when documenting a milestone.

Examiner's advice

"There is no need to exhaustively demonstrate each test, but there should be enough evidence to convince the reader that substantial testing took place. The best projects focus on the more unusual problems that cropped up during developmental testing (getting libraries to work, nuances of programming language, issues with file types) rather than trivial syntax errors."

Pitfalls to avoid when developing your game

Making your game is the fun part of the project, but you need to be careful that you are focussed on attaining what is required to meet the expectations of the mark scheme and do not become side-tracked.

Some considerations to bear in mind:

- There are no marks for graphics. Although you want your game to look good, partly to meet your stakeholder's expectations, you should remember that spending too much time working on graphics is time lost from developing algorithms which gains you marks. It is acceptable for you to source and use sprite sheets. Just remember to provide references to original sources. If you intend to sell your game, you will need to use Creative Commons licensed images.
- There are no marks for creating lots of additional levels or game worlds. You should be aiming to create a "game engine" so that your code is independent of the data it is applied to. This means the code for the first level of your game should also be the code for the second and subsequent levels of your game. Storing the data for the level in collections, data structures or files enables reusable program components. There is no requirement to produce a large number of levels. Often just one will suffice but designed correctly it should not be too difficult to include a couple. Do not spend a long time on designing maps and levels.
- Consider the minimum number of different objects your game requires. For example, you may want to include five different power-ups but are they essential to meeting the success criteria, or could the scope be reduced so that you do not run out of time? Once you have the basic game implemented you can then return to previous milestones and make them better by including more components. There is no requirement to include "boss fights".
- Do not spend a long time playing your game or other games to delay working on tricky algorithms, convincing yourself that you are working! You need to spend time playing games for the research stage of the analysis and playing your game when testing the milestone, but too much time in lessons spent talking and playing will not get the work done! The project can seem overwhelming at times, but you need to keep putting one foot in front of the other.
- Do not leave the development to the last minute. You will be surprised how long it takes to develop even a simple game. You need to have sufficient time to write a good evaluation and you should avoid doing the design retrospectively. It is acceptable to be producing the design for a milestone just before you develop it, folding the design into the development process.

SECTION		DO's		DON'Ts
Agile development	33	Provide evidence of developing each milestone using a development diary approach.	☐	Provide one code listing as evidence of the coded solution without a discussion of the development process. Go back and change your design section.
	34	Include a code listing for the milestone and highlight interesting routines.	☐	
	35	Explain how the milestone was implemented, discussing approaches that were taken, how and why they deviate from the original design.	☐	
Code	36	Produce modular code using procedures, functions and/or methods.	☐	Assume that a data structure or approach you used is obvious to the examiner. Create code for the sake of it if there are suitable library functions you can use. Copy and paste code without references.
	37	Use comments at the beginning of routines and for selection and iterations as a minimum.	☐	
	38	Use sensible variable and data structure names.	☐	
Development testing	39	Test each module for function including the possible program paths.	☐	Forget that games have input validation too preventing the player performing actions that are not permitted.
	40	Test a wide range of situations for each object.		
	41	Provide evidence of the testing, perhaps using a limited number of screen shots.	☐	
Stakeholders	42	Show your completed milestone to a stakeholder for review and capture their comments.	☐	Forget to include your stakeholder in the development process. Remember this is an agile approach, not software development life cycle.
Reflection	43	Review each milestone and discuss what needs to be changed because of play testing.	☐	Be subjective in your review. Hide weaknesses in your code, discuss them instead.
	44	Explain any changes required and any modifications to the design of the solution that result from the stakeholder feedback.	☐	

EVALUATION

Reviewing the project.

In this section, you are discussing **how effective** your project was.

5 marks	Testing to inform the evaluation
15 marks	Evaluation

What to include

- Evidence of your game being played and tested, ideally with a video.
- Discussion of each of the success criteria and whether they were full, partially or not met.
- Discussion of the usability features and whether they were successful, a partial success or a failure.
- Consideration of the limitations and improvements that could be made.
- Discussion of how improvements could be implemented.

Testing to inform the evaluation

In the coded solution section, you performed what is known as "bottom-up" testing. Each module or milestone was tested independently for functionality as it was being developed, but at that stage, you did not test the game as a complete product. Towards the end of a project, a post-development testing phase takes place before the product is shipped.

- Integration testing checks all the individual components work together as a whole.
- Alpha testing assesses to what extent the final product achieves the success criteria.
- Beta testing allows the user to test the game for usability before release.

Your testing to inform the evaluation should consider all these types of tests.

A* TOP TIP

You must include both integration testing by playing all aspects of your game together and usability testing to test the interfaces, input mechanism and difficulty are appropriate.

Evidence

It is important to provide evidence of fully testing your game beyond the simple screenshots you have produced to evidence the completion of a milestone. The examiner will not run your project code. The only evidence they will see of your game in action is what you present here. The best way to evidence your solution is to create a "Let's Play" video of your game being played.

Windows 10 has a built-in feature called Game Bar that will allow you to record your screen. Go to Settings > Gaming on your PC to control the settings for the Game Bar and see the keyboard shortcuts. Alternatively, there are plenty of other products you can use too.

It is important your video evidence is methodical and demonstrates:

- **Function:** The game being played; this does not need to be the whole game but rather a comprehensive selection of its features.
- **Robustness:** In other words, validation of inputs preventing the player exiting the screen, moving through walls, etc. Where there is more than one invalid action, all should be demonstrated - for example, colliding with a wall from the top, bottom, left and right.
- **Usability:** For example, menu options, on-screen prompts or text such as the score, increasing difficulty, etc.

A good approach is to copy your test tables from the design section and add two extra columns to the end of each table; one to record a timestamp of where the test is performed in the video and a second to indicate whether the test was passed or failed. Your product does not need to pass every test. What matters more is that you have good evidence of tests being carried out.

A* TOP TIP

The best evidence covers many eventualities. For example, in a Breakout game, you would need to test the ball hitting a brick on the left, right, top and bottom to be sure it works.

Providing a voice-over that explains what is being tested will help the examiner follow what they are being shown in your video. There is no need to include a script in your project.

Although this section is only worth five marks, it is the evidence of testing for the coded solution and the basis of the evaluation, so its importance should not be under-estimated.

Example of a test table

Milestone 1: Move the player			Evidence	
Test no.	**What is being tested and inputs**	**Expected output**	**Timestamp**	**Pass/Fail**
1	The player spawns on the screen.	The player sprite appears at the bottom-left area of the screen.	0:23	Pass
2	The player can move left with A and right with D.	The player moves left and right at a reasonable speed but cannot leave the screen.	0:27-0:35	Pass
3	An animation is played when the player moves.	The ship sprite changes to bank left and right and idle when no key is pressed.	0:27-0:35	Pass

EVALUATION

Examiner's advice

"It is important that evidence is provided of tests. Where there are several similar tests, it is not necessary to provide a screenshot of all of them, but there should be sufficient evidence to demonstrate the extent to which the system functions.

Example of a voice-over for your Let's Play video

"Test 1. In this test, I am checking the player spawns on the screen in the bottom-left corner of the screen.

Test 2 and 3. I can move the player left and right and the animation changes correctly. I am unable to exit the screen on the left when I reach the edge and continue to hold the A key. I am unable to exit the screen on the right when I reach the edge and continue to hold the D key."

Although a voice-over allows you to talk about your development in more detail, it is also acceptable to provide a series of on-screen annotations instead.

There is no "correct" number of tests you should perform; it will vary hugely from project to project. Your testing needs to be comprehensive but not trivial. For example, if one swarm of aliens spawns correctly, you may want to check a second wave spawns when the last alien is shot and the aliens move a little faster in wave two, but there is no need to test waves three, four and five. If you have about thirty tests in total, that is probably about right.

Weaker projects often fail to test the game adequately. For example, the game might end if an invader hits the player ship. In this example, you would want to test the invader hitting the player both from the left and the right. Although Defold provides collision objects that make this easy to develop, it doesn't mean your collision shape is correct.

Examiner's advice

"Many candidates provide video evidence of their testing, giving appropriate time codes for each test in their documentation; this worked extremely well and left the moderator in no doubt that the system worked as claimed."

Remember, as is the case with all sections of the project, how you evidence your work is up to you. There is no requirement to produce a video. You could choose to use a series of screenshots instead, but that makes it more difficult to illustrate some of the tests you are performing.

A* TOP TIP

For top marks, you should explain how your evidence shows that the success criteria have been met.

Examiner's advice

"Candidates should aim to take each objective listed in their analysis, cross-reference it with the tests they have carried out and discuss how successfully the objective has been met."

Evaluating your game

It is very easy to overlook the importance of the evaluation. Remember, it is worth more marks than the analysis, equal to the design and, combined with the testing, almost as much as the coded solution. Therefore, you need to leave yourself enough time to do this section justice.

At this point, all your development and testing work is complete. It may not be 100% how you envisaged it at the analysis and design stage, but the game is ready to ship! In the gaming industry, there are very tight deadlines to meet to get a product to market. Sometimes, features need to be held back to be released later in patches, updates and sequels.

It is common with games to receive reviews from critics, outlining the positive and negative aspects of the game. Game review channels on YouTube and written reviews on websites such as *IGN* will give you a good indication of the requirements for this part of your report. Consider asking a friend or your user to provide you with a review. That will often give you more to write about because they will see your project from a different perspective, and it can be hard to be truly objective about your game when you have poured your heart and soul into its development.

> **A* TOP TIP**
> A review from your user is not essential but, if done properly, can provide you with a lot to write about in this section to achieve higher marks.

You should copy your success criteria from the analysis section and provide commentary about how successful you were in achieving each of those goals. For each criterion, state whether it was fully met, partially met or not met at all. Also, explain how well the criteria was achieved in each case.

Consider the criticisms from your game review. How could you address these if you had more time? What approaches would be required? If you could release subsequent content (DLC), what would that include? More levels, more power-ups, more weapons? Remember to include the positive aspects too so your evaluation is balanced.

Consider the usability and interface of your product. How could you make the user experience even better? Ideas might include having key bindings for controllers, having a responsive resolution so it can be played on a variety of platforms or portrait/landscape modes for mobile devices.

> **A* TOP TIP**
> Include a discussion about how the usability of the game could be improved. Perhaps you could include options for the player to change the controls, for example.

Options such as pause, save and load could also enhance your game. Maybe the difficulty curve isn't quite right, or it would benefit from having tutorials in the early stages to guide the player.

You should discuss your limitations in detail. Defold is a very capable product for simple games, but there are certainly limitations when it comes to creating more advanced games. You could conduct some simple research into more sophisticated engines such as Unity or Unreal to understand their capabilities. Compare these with your project and think about how these more advanced features might be applied to your work.

A* TOP TIP

Explain how you would address any partially met or unmet criteria with further development if you had time.

It is acceptable not to have met criteria and even to state that you do not know how to approach coding something that proved to be too difficult.

Example of a small section of the evaluation

Criteria		Success	Evaluation
3	Display the score.	Fully met	The score is displayed in the top-left corner. It would be much more interesting if this didn't simply change but counted up to the new score. I could achieve this by introducing a score target variable and increasing the score displayed by 1 in each frame until the score target was reached.
10	Only display a UFO if more than eight aliens are alive.	Partially met	The UFO spawns and can be shot, but it appears completely randomly. I need to introduce another condition to check how many aliens are alive to get this working.
13	There will be two types of alien missile.	Not met	During development, my user suggested this would no longer be necessary because it didn't add much to the game. It was better to focus development time on power-ups instead.

SECTION		DO's		DON'Ts
Post development testing	45	Provide evidence of testing against the test plans you created in the design section.	☐	Produce pages and pages of screenshots. Find a more efficient way of presenting your evidence. Forget that robustness is as important as function. Forget to cross reference to your success criteria, this is known as alpha testing.
	46	Use efficient ways of evidencing the testing. A video is an ideal alternative to screen shots.	☐	
	47	Provide evidence that the game is robust and does not crash or behave unpredictably too easily.	☐	
	48	Consider using a beta test and asking your stakeholder for a review.	☐	
	49	Cross-reference the test evidence against the success criteria from the analysis section to evaluate how well the finished game meets these criteria.	☐	
Usability features	50	Show how the usability features have been tested to make sure they meet the stakeholder needs and industry expectations.	☐	Use evaluative comments that are subjective.
Evaluation	51	Provide a commentary on how well the game matches each of the success criteria.	☐	Include a simple tick list to state each criterion was met. Make comments about how much you enjoyed the project. Forget to say how you might address any of the weaknesses identified in your evaluation.
	52	Comment on any unmet criteria and how these might be approached.	☐	
	53	Comment on any limitations and insurmountable problems you faced.	☐	

Printed in Great Britain
by Amazon

43286169R00035